WHO WOULD YOU DO?

WHO WOULD YOU DO?

Susan Segrest

**THE TOTALLY UNAUTHORIZED
CELEBRITY SEX GAME**

VILLARD / NEW YORK

Library of Congress Cataloging-in-Publication Data

Segrest, Susan.
Who would you do? : the totally unauthorized celebrity sex game /
Susan Segrest.

p. cm.
ISBN 0-8129-6753-4
1. Adult party games. 2. Sexual fantasies. 3. Celebrities.
I. Title: Totally unauthorized celebrity sex game. II. Title.

GV1474 .S44 2003
793.2—dc21   2002033113

Villard Books website address: www.villard.com

Printed in the United States of America on acid-free paper

24689753
First Edition

Book design by Casey Hampton

Although it goes without saying, the author wishes to note for the record that none of the individuals mentioned in the book, living or dead, have consented to making an appearance in her book or her fantasy life.

WHO WOULD YOU DO?

As you go through life you're constantly faced with choices: Big Mac or Whopper? MTV or VH1? Starbucks or Maxwell House? Now imagine if you were faced with the same options in your **sex life**. Only the **choices** were star-studded. **Julia Roberts** or **Gwyneth Paltrow**? **Brad Pitt** or **George Clooney**? **Madonna** or **Jon Bon Jovi**? Think about it. Given these options, **who would you do?** Not a bad scenario, eh?

But what if the choices took an ugly turn from

time to time? For some, having to choose between **Michael Bolton** and **Kenny G** would be hell on earth. What about a roll in the hay with **Martha Stewart** or **Dr. Laura**? Any way you picture it, it's a fate worse than death. However, the first rule of this game is that death is not an option.

I became obsessed with this provocative parlor game about ten years ago. I was sitting in my sister's kitchen. She was stirring a pot of spaghetti; I was drinking a glass of wine and flipping through the newspaper. I turned the page and saw a photo of Bill Clinton and Al Gore, the newly nominated Democratic candidates. Maybe it was curiosity, maybe it was the chardonnay, but I asked her, "Who would you rather have sex with, **Bill** or **Al**?" Without so much as looking up from the stove she answered, "Bill Clinton. Because if a woman came between Al and Tipper it would destroy the Gores' marriage. But I know the Clintons would get through it."

And clearly they have.

That was the beginning of Who Would You Do?—the hypothetical, no-holds-barred, no-celebrity-too-hot and no-rock-star-too-gross question-and-answer game.

I've played this game so often I've begun to think that it's polite conversation to ask people about their sex fantasies. So now it's your turn. Here are the rules:

1. Start out with people you know—at least a little. But remember, it's more fun with people you know a lot. Because even though you can list all of your best friend's trysts and tattoos, you will be amazed at who your buddy wants to take a tumble with.

2. On each page of this book you will be faced with a sexual selection. You have ten seconds to choose your bedmate and confess the reason behind your libidinous liaison. Example: "Even though Michael Bolton looks better with short hair (and Ashley Judd did date him), Kenny G gets my vote because he makes his living with his tongue, lips, and fingers. So how bad could he be in bed?"

3. If you want to make the game really competitive (or just amp up the fun) have your friends write down their answers and mix them all up. Next, take turns reading the names out loud and guessing who said what. The person who most often matches the friends to the chosen celeb sex partner wins.

And remember, you have to pick someone. None of this "I'd rather die." You can say *ick* and *eeeeeew* as much as you like, but you still have to pick your partner.

So now that you know the rules, it's time to get cracking. Have fun!

WALK OF SHAME

Would you rather have an erotic all-nighter with **Tom Cruise**—but the next morning you have to walk home in nothing but his boxers, and along the way you run into your mother, your priest, and your first-grade teacher— or a mere five-minute quickie with **Brad Pitt** but with no public humiliation?

FRIENDS FANTASY

Who would you rather see butt naked every night through your bedroom window: **Monica** or **Phoebe** or **Rachel**?

In which of these naughty novels would you like to be the main character: *Memoirs of a Geisha Gone Bad, Midnight in the Vegetable Garden of the Good and the Sleazy,* or *Angela's Asses*?

EROTICA

MULTIPLE MODEL CHOICE

Gisele Bundchen, Naomi Campbell, Laetitia Casta, Cindy Crawford, Heidi Klum, Elle Macpherson, Kate Moss, Molly Sims, and Christy Turlington all want you and only you. Unfortunately, there's only so much of your precious self to go around. Pick one hot model for a random quickie, one for a romantic weekend away, and one for a walk down the aisle.

LATE-SHOW LUST

It's bedtime, but you just aren't ready to go to sleep. So who would you rather have talk dirty to you: **Jay Leno, David Letterman, Jon Stewart,** or **Conan O'Brien**?

Some people like to let the stars guide their sexual selections. **Aries** is an adventurer. So whether it is group sex, light S & M, or some other exotic pastime, this sign enjoys trying new things—and new people. You have thirty seconds to make your rapid-fire selections.

Gary Oldman or **George Benson?**

Mariah Carey or **Emmylou Harris?**

Andrew Lloyd Webber or **Tim Curry?**

Reese Witherspoon or **Kate Hudson?**

Hugh Hefner or **Luther Vandross?**

Mandy Moore or **Tracy Chapman?**

Buddy Ebsen or **Pete Rose?**

Doris Day or **Julie Christie?**

Michael York or **Leon Russell?**

Catherine Keener or **Leeza Gibbons?**

ASTROLOGICAL
AROUSAL

Would you rather do **Samantha** at a
Chelsea sex club, make out with **Carrie**
at a celeb-filled TriBeCa party, have a
lusty desktop liaison with **Miranda** at
a Wall Street law firm, or lock yourself
in a SoHo gallery with nothing but
a paintbrush and **Charlotte** as your
canvas?

SEX AND THE CITY
SCENARIO

NAUGHTY NIGHT/ DIRTY DAY

You could have a day at a nude beach with **Ben Affleck** or a night in the dark with **Matt Damon**. Which would you pick?

You have to compete in a naked couple skate with **Tonya Harding** as your partner or find yourself in a prison shower with **Amy Fisher** rubbing you down. Which would you choose?

SCANDAL BABE SHOWDOWN

HAWAII FIVE-OOOOOO!

While relaxing at one of those dime-a-dozen Hawaiian beachside sex parties, you notice a line of lusty women all waiting to do the limbo. What's curious is that they all seem to be wearing miniskirts and no panties. Hmmmm. They beg you to be the judge, and since you live to give, you agree. After you've seen everything, and we mean *everything*, it comes down to a tie between these five foxy femmes: **Cameron Diaz, Jennifer Lopez, Kate Hudson, Kirsten Dunst,** and **Keri Russell**. Who will be awarded the winning lay?

You wake up in the middle of the night to find **Hugh Grant** and **Hugh Jackman** standing at the foot of your bed begging you for sex. But you can say yes to only one. Who would you do?

ROOM WITH A HUGH

You are a guest on *The View*. You chat, you flirt, you promote your blockbuster movie and then, one by one, each of the hosts slips you a little note inviting you back to her dressing room. Who would you rather do: **Joy Behar, Star Jones, Meredith Vieira,** or **Barbara Walters**?

ROMP WITH A VIEW

LOSING YOUR RELIGION

Who would you do: the **Pope** or the **Dalai Lama**?

NASTY THURSDAY NIGHTS

Somehow a case of Viagra, a container of Spanish fly, and a couple of bottles of tequila accidentally got mixed into the chili that **Will** and **Grace** were serving for dinner. Oops. Suddenly there's an apartment full of horny people and only you to give these poor folks some relief. But in what order do you pass out your sexual healing? Give everyone, including **Will Truman, Grace Adler, Jack McFarland, Karen Walker,** and **Rosario,** a number.

LOVE MATCH

All of these tantalizing tennis divas dare you to give them your hardest serve. Which do you accept: **Anna Kournikova, Venus Williams,** or **Lindsay Davenport**?

PRIVATE PEEP SHOW

It's your *Basic Instinct* moment and both **Sharon Stone** and **Michael Douglas** are trying to distract you with some full-frontal flashing. Where do your eyes go?

You are standing by the dessert table at your office holiday party, stuffing your pockets with sweet treats for later, when a woman approaches and says, "Is that a pignoli cookie in your pocket or are you just happy to see me?" Embarrassed, you tell her that you're *very* excited. That's when she invites you for a no-holds-barred booty session in the broom closet. Who would you want this bold babe to be—**Connie Chung** or **Diane Sawyer?**

TASTY TEMPTATION

MUSICAL MOJO

Who would you rather play strip poker with: **Sean "P. Diddy" Combs** or **Kenneth "Babyface" Edmonds**?

Taurus is forceful, romantic, jealous, and very, very oral. In this speed round, you have thirty seconds to choose your bullish babes.

Valerie Bertinelli or **Carmen Electra?**
Joey Lawrence or **Jack Klugman?**
Jessica Lange or **Jessica Alba?**
Lance Bass or **Randy Travis?**
Bianca Jagger or **Donatella Versace?**
Burt Bacharach or **Harvey Keitel?**
Ann-Margret or **Hayley Mills?**
Engelbert Humperdinck or **Pete Seeger?**
Roma Downey or **Sheena Easton?**
Don Rickles or Willie Nelson?

ASTROLOGICAL
AROUSAL

You are in the middle of a hot-'n'-heavy sex session with, er, yourself when in walk **Angela Lansbury, Debbie Reynolds,** and **Billy Graham**. "I can explain," you stammer, trying to come up with a perfectly reasonable justification as to why your pants are around your ankles. But it's no use. Who would you rather have been caught by?

SOLO-SESSION SNAFU

NAUGHTY NEWS

Would you prefer to dress **Dan Rather** up in S & M gear and spank his naked butt every night for the next year

OR

have **Peter Jennings** dress you up in S & M gear and spank your naked butt every night for the next year?

PUBLIC FLAME OR SECRET SHAME

Would you rather be **Meg Ryan**'s secret sex slave (but she never acknowledges you in public) or **Julia Roberts**'s man about town (including her date to the Oscars) but not get any action with her between the sheets?

Emeril Lagasse wants to lay you down on his stainless steel prep counter and tenderize every inch of your body. (Bam!) **Bobby Flay** has offered to baste your bare flesh with an orange marmalade beurre blanc sauce and then really get cooking with you. **Jamie Oliver** just wants to pour on a little olive oil and start feasting. Who would you do?

KITCHEN CONFIDENTIAL

GOLDEN GO-GO GIRLS

Who would you rather see perform a pole dance in a G-string at your local strip club—**Rue McClanahan, Betty White,** or **Bea Arthur?**

It's another boring day at the office. Just like clockwork, you're asked to strip naked as a jaybird and sit on your boss's lap to take dictation. Then your phone rings and you get the same request from your other boss. (They are so gosh-darn competitive.) Who do you service: **Queen Elizabeth** or **Dame Edna**?

REGAL RAUNCH

FRISKY FETE

Quick, create the perfect sex party. In under thirty seconds, name five celebs, five real people, and one great location—then describe your ideal orgy.

For example: *David Duchovny, George Clooney, Hugh Jackman, Gary Sinise, and The Rock, along with my FedEx guy, my UPS guy, my trainer, my college boyfriend, and the cute waiter at that café around the corner all meet on Waikiki for a weekend devoted to pleasuring me. When they aren't working to bring me to orgasm they must wear hula skirts and leis and do little dances for me.*

Times are tough, and you must make some extra cash to pay the bills. A friend passes you an ad that reads "Celebrity Seeks Nude Pet Trainer. You: stand around in the buff while teaching my four Rottweilers how to behave. I: get to watch." You think, "There is no way in hell I'm going to risk getting my ass chewed off (or worse); I am so insulted that my friend even thought of me for this sick, sick job." But then you read that it pays $1,000 an hour. And, well, everyone has a price. Who would you prefer to work for: **Dr. Joyce Brothers, Joel Grey,** or **Julia Child**?

HELP WANTED

TAKING THE EXPRESS

You're riding in an elevator when you see that **Martin Sheen** and **Ed Harris** are standing mere inches in front of you. You are far too cool to ask for autographs, but you want to acknowledge their creative contributions in some small way. So whose butt do you give a strong, supportive squeeze?

ANGEL ACTION

Would you rather have a devilish ménage à quatre with **Lucy Liu, Cameron Diaz,** and **Drew Barrymore** or a frisky flashback with **Farrah Fawcett, Kate Jackson,** and **Jaclyn Smith**?

The Rock and **Stone Cold Steve Austin** both want to get you down for the mount. Which one will you choose and which one will you tell, as The Rock might say, "to drink a big old tall glass of good-bye juice"?

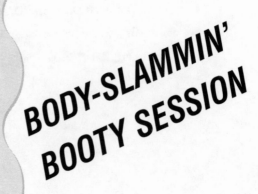

BODY-SLAMMIN' BOOTY SESSION

GENDER BENDER

You are a delightful, handsome, rich, charming, forty-something-but-looks-younger gay man. All you want in life is to marry (in Vermont) another handsome man, adopt a cute little baby, and live happily ever after in your downtown loft. So far Mr. Right hasn't appeared, but, bizarrely, each of the following women has offered to undergo a sex change in order to be with you. Who would you choose as your female-to-male mate: **Bernadette Peters, Cher,** or **Laura Bush**?

TROUBLING TRYST

Would you rather lick Cheez Whiz off **Danny DeVito**'s bare body or give **Howard Stern** a nude lap dance on national television?

Your choice: one night of up-against-the-wall, in-the-shower, down-on-the-floor, and swinging-from-the-chandeliers crazy sex with **Benjamin Bratt** or an entire year of sweet, soft, bedtime kisses and all-through-the-night cuddles from **Jesse L. Martin**. Who would you pick?

LAW AND DISORDERLY CONDUCT

Geminis are sexpots who love to multitask in bed. Some tawdry twins also like to swing both ways. In this thirty-second speed round, pick your cosmic connection.

Drew Carey or **Danny Aiello?**
Gena Rowlands or **Pam Grier?**
Al Franken or **Martin Landau?**
Peri Gilpin or **Brooke Shields?**
Gregory Harrison or **Parker Stevenson?**
Julianna Margulies or **Amanda Pays?**
Bob Hope or **Boz Scaggs?**
Dixie Carter or **Anne Heche?**
Hank Williams Jr. or **Johnny Paycheck?**
Sally Kellerman or **Barbara Bush?**

ASTROLOGICAL AROUSAL

CLEAN LIVING

You're gonna get it. You've tried scrubbing and soaking, but you still can't get the laundry fresh enough for your dominatrix. Who do you most want to punish you: **Martha Stewart** or **Dr. Laura**?

BRITISH BOYS

You nip over the pond for a quiet weekend away, but alas, there's no rest for the incredibly hot. **Elton John** pounds on your hotel door, desperate to be your rocket man, and **Rupert Everett** sneaks in through the bedroom window swearing that if you give him a chance, he'll prove that he's the next best thing to heaven in the sack. Who will you disappoint?

When you want to do the dirty with a celeb on-line you have to use your best pickup label. But what to choose? We know from personal experience that all the good screen names are taken. So here's an easy way:

Take the name of your best body part plus your favorite sex position, lucky number, and town name. This creates, for example, assdoggie69newyork. Play around with it until you find the one that best expresses your erotic electronic persona.

CYBER-SEX HANDLE

The **Bionic Woman,** Jaime Sommers, offers to demonstrate the amazing sexual powers she was given in the lab, and **Wonder Woman,** Diana Prince, whispers that she's desperate to slip off that little skintight superhero number and, while still wearing her knee-high boots, show you what her magic lasso is really used for. Who would you do?

1970s SUPERFEMMES

SCANDAL SCENARIO

You've stopped on the side of the highway in L.A. to use the rest room when **George Michael** taps on the door and propositions you for some fast love. You, of course, say yes.

OR

You're minding your own business just walking the dark, mean streets of L.A. in nothing but your torn fishnets, pleather miniskirt, and glittery tube top when a Town Car pulls up and **Hugh Grant** propositions you. You, of course, get in.

Which slutty scandal scenario would you choose?

BIKER BOOTY

Your Harley has broken down in the middle of the desert at sunset, and there is no rescue in sight. You're afraid you'll be cozying up to a cactus until suddenly, both **Gary Busey** and **Mickey Rourke** come blazing in and offer to give you the ride of your life. Whose hog will you mount?

These ladies are feeling frisky and risky, and each is praying that you'll want to join her for some carnal cavorting. **Heather Locklear** is skinny-dipping in the *Melrose Place* communal pool. **Heather Graham** is having a *Boogie Nights* moment and is roller-skating naked around your limousine. Who would you do?

BLONDE
AMBITION

Things aren't looking good. A bipolar billionaire has decided he wants to steal a space shuttle, take over a Vegas casino, and, while he's at it, use his girlfriend's psychic power to foretell his criminal future. There is only one man who can derail this attempt at world domination. Well, actually five men. Which James Bond would you pick to protect the planet and, of course, have the obligatory post–saving-the-world ultrasmooth sex scene with: **Sean Connery, George Lazenby** (sure, he was only in one movie but it's only kind to include him), **Roger Moore, Timothy Dalton,** or **Pierce Brosnan?**

JAMES BONDAGE

IF THIS STADIUM'S A-ROCKIN' . . .

In interview after interview, **Madonna** and **Jon Bon Jovi** can't stop talking about the sweet, sweet love they feel for you. (Your lips, your eyes, your handy knowledge of world events— what's not to worship?) But the time has come. You have to pick one and, well, prepare to get out a restraining order on the other. Who will you choose?

Prince William, the tastiest slice of white bread since Wonder hit the shelves, has asked you to take a rockin' ride on the back of his polo pony. But the singer sporadically known as **Prince** wants to party in your pants like it's 1999. Who would you do?

RANDY ROYALS

LADY LOVE

Get some flashback action. Who would you do: **Ethel Merman** or **Shelley Winters**?

SUGAR DADDY-O

You've just graduated from the Anna Nicole Smith Institute with a major in the Ancient Art of Seducing Rich Older Men and a minor in the complexities of Inheritance Tax. (You've also invested in collagen-injected lips, store-bought double-D's, and triple-processed blond hair.) Now that you are ready for the big time, which of these gazillionaires would you like to wrangle: **Ross Perot, Donald Trump,** or **Bill Gates?**

You have a major foot fetish and are
eager for some indecent toe exposure.
Whose tootsies do you want to tongue:
Imelda Marcos's or **Marla Maples**'s?

ARCH AROUSAL

Sex with a **Cancer** is slow, sweet, and unbearably erotic. In this thirty-second speed round, pick which celebs you want to crawl around with.

Cyndi Lauper or **Meryl Streep**?
Don Knotts or **Don Henley**?
Edie Falco or **Frances McDormand**?
Jan-Michael Vincent or **Kris Kristofferson**?
Phoebe Cates or **Kristi Yamaguchi**?
Forest Whitaker or **James Brolin**?
Sela Ward or **Mel Harris**?
Dan Aykroyd or **Brian Dennehy**?
Lorrie Morgan or **Missy Elliott**?

ASTROLOGICAL
AROUSAL

MY THREE BUNS

Emilio Estevez, Jeff Bridges, and **Colin Hanks,** the sexy sons of three Hollywood superstars, want you to do the *Buns of Steel* video naked while they watch. Which one will you choose to view your cheeky workout?

CARNAL CLASS REUNION

Since high school graduation your skin's cleared up, your body's buffed up, and your bank account's booming. So this year's class reunion is one you want to attend. Who would you rather bring as your date: **Michael Michele, Sarah Jessica Parker, Britney Spears,** or **Parker Posey?** And postreunion, which of these lovely ladies would you like to be caught doing on the hood of your Hummer?

Austin Powers wants you to lick his hygiene-challenged teeth, **Fat Bastard** wants you to curl up next to his sweaty bod and kiss his big ol' belly, **Mini-Me** wants you to play "This Little Piggy" on his toes with your mouth, and **Dr. Evil** wants you to be his naughty nurse in training. Yeah, baby! Who do you do and who would you tell to just *behave*?

THE SPY WHO GAGGED ME

GREAT DAMES

You're on the tube in London just trying to read the *Economist* when suddenly you feel a hand gently stroking your left inner thigh. You turn and see **Dame Maggie Smith** smiling at you seductively. Then, not to be outdone, **Dame Judi Dench** slips to your other side and leans in for a big, hot, wet French kiss. Who do you go home with?

It is two A.M. and you're trying to get to sleep, but your musically minded bedmate desperately wants to get you in the mood. Who would heat you up and who would leave you cold? **Chris Isaak** (singing "Baby Did a Bad Bad Thing"), **Jennifer Lopez** (singing "Let's Get Loud"), **Rob Thomas** and **Carlos Santana** (performing "Smooth"), or **Melissa Etheridge** (singing "I'm the Only One")?

SWEET DREAMS

HEEEEEEERE'S JOHNNY

In their prime, who would you most want to mess around with: **Johnny Carson, Johnny Cash,** or **Johnny Mathis?**

You're at a sex party playing a perfectly innocent game of Strip Twister with a group of hot female celebrities. Everyone's close to falling into a naked heap of bodies on the mat when you spin the wheel and land on "left butt cheek red." As you make your move, you slip and fall on a very famous face. Does it belong to **Julia Roberts, Gwen Stefani, Ashley Judd,** or **Janet Reno?**

PARTY FAVORS

GAME-SHOW SEDUCTION

You've won the big-screen TV *and* the Spiegel-catalog gift certificate, but during the commercial break, the host slyly sidles up to you and lets you know there is more to come. "For a real prize," he says, "follow me to my trailer for a bawdy bonus round." Quickly checking to see if you have any morals, then remembering that you lost them long ago, you tell him you'll do it. Who would you rather it be: **Pat Sajak, Alex Trebek,** or **Bob Barker**?

You're in trouble now. **Kelly Ripa** thinks you are hers and hers alone. But **Katie Couric** is telling all of America that *she's* your main squeeze. Who do you acknowledge?

MORNING MAYHEM

You're a foxy bookstore owner who has an unusual marketing plan. In exchange for giving certain books great coverage in the store window, you get erotic attention from featured authors. But you have a dilemma: two of your regulars, **John Irving** and **John Updike,** have both stopped in to service your account. Who do you do?

THE WRITE STUFF

MEN OF MADONNA

Which of these boy toys would you rather play with: **Sean Penn, Warren Beatty, Carlos Leon,** or **Guy Ritchie**?

BODACIOUS TA-TAS

In whose ample bosom would you like to get lost: **Dolly Parton**'s or **Pamela Anderson**'s?

AFTER THE LOVIN'

It's the 1970s and you must have sex with all of these celebs and you must listen to one of these love songs while doing it. Match each of these celebs—**Richard Nixon, Neil Diamond, Carol Burnett, Flip Wilson,** and **John Ritter**—to the background sex song: "I Honestly Love You" by Olivia Newton-John, "You Light Up My Life" by Debby Boone, "Do That to Me One More Time" by the Captain & Tennille, "Precious and Few" by Climax, and "Always and Forever" by Heatwave.

Leo likes to be the boss in the bedroom and loves action, action, action. In this thirty-second speed round, pick the cats that make you roar.

Kate Beckinsale or **Aimee Mann**?
Kevin Spacey or **Billy Bob Thornton**?
Natasha Henstridge or **Stephanie Seymour**?
Mario Van Peebles or **Antonio Banderas**?
Isaac Hayes or **Robert Plant**?
Gillian Anderson or **Loni Anderson**?
Al Roker or **Don Imus**?
Angela Bassett or **Angie Harmon**?
Mel Tillis or **David Crosby**?
Princess Anne or **Rosanna Arquette**?

ASTROLOGICAL AROUSAL

CHEMICAL
REACTION

There was a tragic accident in the lab, and suddenly you find yourself shrinking from six feet tall to six inches tall. The good news is that **Lauryn Hill** and **Lauren Holly** both want you to be their little pocket rocket. Who do you choose?

WHICH WACKO JACKO?

Both **Michael Jackson** and **Janet Jackson** have offered to instruct a hands-on class about normal, healthy, all-American sexual behavior. Who do you choose to be your teacher?

Whoopi Goldberg just purchased a new trampoline and she's invited you over for a birthday-suit bounce-athon, but you already have an invitation for a swanky swing on **Billy Crystal**'s jungle gym. Who do you disappoint?

PLAYGROUND
PASSION

BOY, THE WAY GLENN MILLER PLAYED . . .

All in the Family flashback. Who would you do, **Archie** or **Edith Bunker?**

Gillian Anderson still believes that the truth is out there and is convinced that she will find it in your pants. **Julianne Moore** just wants to get into your pants and doesn't need some lame excuse to do it. Who would you do?

TAWDRY TITIANS

MEN DOWN UNDER

Three saucy Aussies, **Heath Ledger, Guy Pearce,** and **Russell Crowe,** are available for the following amorous activities: a fun-filled day on a nude beach with a Polaroid camera, an indecent weekend in the wine country, or two weeks in the outback making love among the livestock. Who do you pick for each adventure?

Maybe it's their all-natural, girl-next-door look, but you are obsessed with having **Joan Collins** and **Joan Rivers** participate in a private wet T-shirt contest. Unfortunately, there isn't enough time for both of them to put on a show. Who would you pick?

MOANING FOR JOAN

DIRTY DETECTIVES

It's Malibu in the early seventies. You're on the beach wearing your favorite outfit (fringed halter top, cutoff jean shorts) when suddenly a couple of thugs try to rough you up. Who would you choose to save you: manly **Joe Mannix** or the weather-beaten but winsome **Jim Rockford**?

LESBIAN LUST

You are so damn sexy that you have your pick of the lesbian litter. Choose one of these famous femmes for a dinner date, a one-night stand, a romantic weekend away, and a life partner: **k. d. lang, Sandra Bernhard, Ellen DeGeneres, Rosie O'Donnell**.

Lord knows you try to stay out of trouble, but somehow you've gotten mixed up in a make-sex-videos-with-celebs-then-blackmail-them-for-millions crime ring. Your next assignment is either **Tiger Woods** or **James Woods**. Who do you seduce?

HOT AND UNCENSORED

You're backstage at the Academy Awards when your baby wins the big one—and proceeds to give *quite* the acceptance speech. Who would you give a wild and wanton congratulatory boink: **Sally Field, Cuba Gooding Jr., Roberto Benigni, Tom Hanks,** or **Gwyneth Paltrow**?

YOU LIKE ME

OTHERWORLDLY ROMPS

Although **Buffy the Vampire Slayer** (Sarah Michelle Gellar) and **Angel** (David Boreanaz) still burn, burn, burn for each other, they've decided that you're giving off some spicy heat as well. Who do you do?

SECRETS OF YOUR SEXUAL PAST

For some reason you feel compelled to confess the erotic indiscretions of your youth to an unsuspecting new lover. Which of the following scenarios would you be most likely to admit?

a. One summer back in 1981 you drank a few too many Cuba Libres while staying in Havana and wound up doing the dirty with **Fidel Castro** and a half dozen men from his army.

b. One wild night in Texas you made it with the entire **Dallas Cowboys** team in the middle of the stadium.

c. To pay your way through college you took a job at Hooters and made extra money after hours stripping for **Maury Povich**.

Slow-handed **Virgo** knows each and every last detail about being a sensual and liberated lover, so keep that in mind as you pick your passion playthings in this thirty-second speed round.

Steve Guttenberg or **Scott Hamilton**?
Marlee Matlin or **Twiggy**?
Mark Harmon or **Rick Springfield**?
Lily Tomlin or **Jo Anne Worley**?
Sam Neill or **Tom Skerritt**?
Jada Pinkett Smith or **Gloria Estefan**?
David Soul or **Ed Begley Jr.**?
Fiona Apple or **Shari Belafonte**?
Billy Ray Cyrus or **Richard Marx**?
Kristy McNichol or **Rebecca DeMornay**?

ASTROLOGICAL
AROUSAL

TEACHER'S PET

The bad news is that you absolutely suck at gym class. The good news? Two new instructors, **Gabrielle Reece** and **Steffi Graf,** are eager to help you be all that you can be. Who do you choose?

TV TWOSOME TRYST

You are invited to a ménage à trois with **Felix** and **Oscar** or **Laverne** and **Shirley**. Who's it gonna be?

In under thirty seconds, take these five items—hot candle wax, a feather boa, a blindfold, a silk scarf, and a chain saw—and these five celebs—**John Goodman, Macy Gray, Adam Sandler, Kenneth Branagh,** and **Brandy**—and create a happy little sex romp.

CREATE YOUR OWN SAUCY STORY

The time machine takes you back to a junior high school party circa 1978. You give the Coke bottle a spin and it lands on one of the following lust objects: **David Cassidy** or **Shaun Cassidy**. Who would you most want to smooch?

SPIN THE BOTTLE

BIZARRE BONUS QUESTION

You're dating one of the following celebrities, who happens to have a thing for butt-naked yoga sessions. Who would you rather watch do the Downward Dog: **Sting, Shirley MacLaine,** or **Deepak Chopra**?

BIG BAD BALLS

You're the ump at a pro tennis tournament and **Pete Sampras, Andre Agassi,** and **John McEnroe** have all been very, very bad boys on the court. In order to get to the semifinals they must prove to you just how sorry they are. Who do you start with?

GET YOUR MOTOR RUNNING

Dale Earnhardt Jr. and **Jeff Gordon** are both, literally, hell on wheels. Who would you choose to rev your erotic engines?

SHE'S GOT THE BEAT

Both the **Go-Go's** and the **Spice Girls** are in front of your house, dancing bare-naked, desperate for your attention. Who do you disappoint?

Imagine that the following song titles are sex positions. Which one would you most want to try?

a. "Like a Virgin" by Madonna
b. "Bootylicious" by Destiny's Child
c. "Wind Beneath My Wings" by Bette Midler
d. "Ain't No Mountain High Enough" by Diana Ross
e. "Karma Chameleon" by Culture Club
f. "Fly Me to the Moon" by Frank Sinatra

KAMA TUNE-TRA

WICKED WESTERNS

You're on the set of *Butch Cassidy and the Sundance Kid* and **Paul Newman** and **Robert Redford** are both giving you smoldering X-rated stares. But you can have only one of them. Who would you do?

MOTHER KNOWS BEST

These three ladies know how to do everything right: make the perfect bed, cook the perfect meal, and always look fresh as a daisy doing it. Would you do: **June Cleaver** from *Leave It to Beaver* (while husband Ward is still at work), **Marge Simpson** from *The Simpsons* (while trying not to mess up that big blue beehive hairdo), or **Harriet Nelson** of *The Adventures of Ozzie and Harriet* (while hiding from her hot teen sons)?

YADA, YADA, YADA

Every member of this neurotic New York foursome wants to get frisky with you. But in addition to major sack time, each has one little thing you must do: **Jerry** wants you to be the butt of his jokes in his nightly stand-up routine. **Elaine** insists that you go out dancing with her every night—in public. **Kramer** requires that you stay in his apartment 24/7, and, not that there's anything wrong with it, **George** expects you to spend every weekend with his parents. Who would you do?

Ozzy Osbourne, Kid Rock, Gene Sim-
mons, and Marilyn Manson have all
been sending you sweet, flirtatious
e-mails, begging to take you out on a
romantic first date you'll never forget.
Who do you dare to say yes to?

OFF THEIR
ROCKERS

Librans love a lot of foreplay, relish some dirty talk, and have plenty of staying power. In this thirty-second speed round, pick your cosmic companions.

Catherine Deneuve or **Annette Funicello**?
John Lithgow or **Jon Favreau**?
Melissa Sue Anderson or **Pam Dawber**?
Yo-Yo Ma or **Oliver North**?
Linda Hamilton or **Kevin Sorbo**?
Ray Charles or **Luciano Pavarotti**?
Elisabeth Shue or **Fran Drescher**?
Wyclef Jean or **Angela Lansbury**?
Marie Osmond or **Gwen Stefani**?
Jeff Conaway or **Jeff Goldblum**?

ASTROLOGICAL AROUSAL

GENDER BENDER

Boy George and **RuPaul** are, for some unknown reason, both flashing their butt cleavage at you. Where do you look?

The time machine is fired up and ready for transport. All you have to do is make a decision. Which commander in chief would you want to tie you to the bedpost in the Lincoln Bedroom? Pick anyone from **George Washington** to **George W.**

PRIME PRESIDENTS

SEX WITH THE EX

Which of these former couples would you want to do the dirty with: **Michael Jackson** and **Lisa Marie Presley** or **Woody Allen** and **Mia Farrow**?

You've just moved into a sprawling eight-bedroom home, but the realtor neglected to inform you that it's located in a clothing-optional community and your neighbor loves to mow the lawn in the buff. Who would you rather see riding a John Deere sans clothing: **David Hasselhoff, Melissa Gilbert, Lorenzo Lamas,** or **Valerie Perrine?**

NAKED NEIGHBOR

MEN IN THE MORNING

The alarm is going off, but you just need one more good-morning snuggle before you face the day. In whose arms would you rather wake up: **Regis Philbin**'s or **Matt Lauer**'s?

Who would you like to get raunchy with in the White House Rose Garden: **Laura Bush, Hillary Clinton, Nancy Reagan,** or **Eleanor Roosevelt**?

FRISKY FIRST
LADIES

DIRTY DOCTORS

Here's the bad news: you've broken both your legs in a terrible accident and it is going to be months before you're on your feet again. The good news: one of these TV docs is going to be by your side 24/7 to nurse you back to health. Who would you want to fulfill your passion prescription: **Dr. John Carter** (Noah Wyle on *ER*), **Doogie Howser, M.D.** (Neil Patrick Harris), **Dr. Luka Kovac** (Goran Visnjic on *ER*), **Trapper John, M.D.** (Pernell Roberts), or **Marcus Welby, M.D.** (Robert Young)?

COUNTRY CUTIES

Shania Twain wants you to impress her (much) with your sexual prowess, but **Faith Hill** also wants to share this kiss with you in the sack. Whose boudoir would you bounce around in?

Jason Sehorn and Joe Namath are both throwing passes your way. Whose will complete?

NEW YORK GRIDIRON GOODIES

TOM'S CATS

Nicole Kidman, Penélope Cruz, and **Mimi Rogers** have all had intimate moments with Tom Cruise. But don't let that put you off. Which one of these women would you like to get carnal with?

If you were to die in bed while having sex with a married man and the news was going to land on the cover of every tabloid, who would you want as your infamous final passion partner: **Jude Law** or **Freddie Prinze Jr.**?

THE YEAR'S BIGGEST SEX SCANDAL

LOVE YOU, LOVER

You've seen their video, now pick your passion partner: **Pamela Anderson** or **Tommy Lee?**

LIGHTS, CAMERA, ACTION HERO

You've just been cast as the female lead in a big blockbuster movie. Since women have so much power in Hollywood, they are letting you choose your leading man. Who's it gonna be: **Sylvester Stallone, Jet Li, Arnold Schwarzenegger, Bruce Willis, Jackie Chan, Kurt Russell, Colin Farrell,** or **Mel Gibson**?

Scorpio rules the astrological house of sex and likes exploring every aspect of it with high velocity. In this thirty-second speed round, pick your cosmic companions:

Goldie Hawn or **Bo Derek?**
Adam Ant or **Charles Bronson?**
Maria Shriver or **Grace Slick?**
Ted Turner or **Bob Hoskins?**
Helen Reddy or **Bonnie Raitt?**
Dwight Yoakam or **Lyle Lovett?**
Kate Jackson or **Kate Capshaw?**
Sam Waterston or **Martin Scorsese?**
MacKenzie Phillips or **Rickie Lee Jones?**
Jonathan Winters or **Dick Smothers?**

ASTROLOGICAL AROUSAL

COFFEE, TEA, OR ME?

You are flying first-class and the flight attendants—**Christina Aguilera, Kim Cattrall, Jennifer Love Hewitt,** and **Elizabeth Hurley**—are first-class babes too. Which of these lovely ladies would you lure into joining the mile-high club?

APOCALYPSE NOW

We were always scared this could happen. **John Wayne Bobbitt** and **Joey Buttafuoco** are the only two men left on earth. Who do you do?

It's the 1960s and you find yourself taking a vacation at an all-nude cattle ranch with **Sophia Loren** and **Elizabeth Taylor**. Who do you offer to ride?

SEXPOT PARTNERS

THE PERFECT PORN

As a very busy actress in the adult film industry, you have four new skin flicks scheduled for back-to-back shooting: *Hothouse Ho, Deflowered in the Shower, Vaseline Vixen,* and *Frustrated Housewife Gets a Special Delivery*. The problem? Deciding who is your best costar for each movie. Your options? **Ted Koppel, Chris Rock, Matthew Broderick,** and **Billy Bob Thornton**.

It's Saturday night and you're driving around looking for a good time. At the strip mall you find not one but two topless female comedy clubs. **Margaret Cho** is performing at one, and at the other, **Kathy Griffin** is putting on a big show. Where do you pay your eighteen-dollar cover, with two-drink minimum?

FUNNY LADY

MEN IN BED

As you long suspected, every damn one of your coworkers is an alien and every damn one wants to take you back to the mother ship. Talk about bad luck. Who would be man enough to keep you here on earth: **Will Smith** or **Tommy Lee Jones**?

Would you rather have front-row seats to an all-nude *NSYNC concert (and get a full-color video of the event to show your friends) or have group sex with the **Backstreet Boys**?

BOY TOYS

CREATE YOUR
OWN SAUCY
STORY

In under thirty seconds, take these five items—a dog collar, an Elvis bobble-head doll, three sets of Mardi Gras beads, a video camera, and a hot-air balloon—and these five celebs—**Lucy Lawless, Joaquin Phoenix, Denis Leary, David Hyde Pierce,** and **J. K. Rowling**—and create a happy little sex romp.

Dick Butkus and **Martin Mull** have asked you to join them in a vigorous rendition of the Funky Chicken—which they both use as foreplay. Who do you say yes to?

POULTRY PASSIONS

DAUNTING DECISIONS

You're at a sex party playing a lusty game called Pass the Peppermint Stick with **Danny Bonaduce, Paula Abdul, Tori Spelling, Tom Green,** and **Tara Reid**. Who are you going to stick it to?

If you were to die in bed while having sex with a married woman and the news was going to land on the cover of every tabloid, who would you prefer as your infamous final passion partner: **Vanessa Williams** or **Uma Thurman**?

THE YEAR'S SECOND-BIGGEST SEX SCANDAL

TOTAL DOLLS

After a tough day at the office, you deserve some relaxation. So you get out your doll collection, quickly take off all their clothes (and yours, of course), and do a little fantasy role-playing. Suddenly, without any warning, **G.I. Joe** and **Ken** transform from being small and made out of hard plastic to being hard in that full-grown-man kind of way. Who would you do?

Sagittarius knows exactly what to do in bed and loves a gleefully erotic partner. In this thirty-second speed round, pick your cosmic companions.

Susan Dey or **Marisa Tomei**?
Tom Waits or **Tom Hulce**?
Jamie Lee Curtis or **JoBeth Williams**?
Dionne Warwick or **Tina Turner**?
Garry Shandling or **Andy Williams**?
Katie Holmes or **Christina Aguilera**?
Keith Richards or **Brenda Lee**?
Ed Koch or **Ed Harris**?
Cathy Lee Crosby or **Cathy Rigby**?
Tim Conway or **Don Johnson**?

ASTROLOGICAL AROUSAL

FANTASY FICTION

Once again, **Julie Andrews** tells you to "put your hands up against the wall, spread your legs, and get ready to be frisked." Then she runs her hands over and under your clothes, looking for concealed weapons. This is an odd request, really, since you are just the doorman in her building. But whatever gets the Christmas tips. A few hours later, **Warren Beatty** asks you to do the same thing for him. Which do you prefer?

MUSCLE GIRLS

Forget high-speed car chases and exotic martial arts—**Angelina Jolie** and **Michelle Yeoh** have invited you to participate in some good old-fashioned hand-to-hand hot combat. Who do you disappoint?

MATRIX MAMBO

Who would you like to have futuristic, slow-motion, technology-enhanced sex with: **Keanu Reeves** or **Laurence Fishburne**?

The stadium's sold out. The band's onstage. You're screaming your head off with excitement when suddenly the lead singer pulls you out of the crowd, grinds his pelvis against you, and begs you to come backstage after the show to party with the whole gang. Which group would you do: **Van Halen, Bon Jovi, Aerosmith,** or **Guns N' Roses**?

BIG-HAIR BOOTY

LUSTY AND LIVE FROM NEW YORK

Be honest: you've spent more Saturday nights watching TV than actually getting any action—so it's only natural that you start fantasizing about your small-screen best friends. Who would you do: **Roseanne Roseannadanna, Opera Man, Church Lady,** or all of the **Coneheads**?

Shedding all modesty, **Joan Jett, Sheryl Crow, Chrissie Hynde,** and **Courtney Love** have all offered to give you a black-tie *only*, randy little concert. Who do you pick?

ROCKIN' YOU, BABY

MARRIED TO THE MOB

You just can't stop playing the ponies, so you're into the family for fifty large. The bosses say you can work off your debt in bed—you just have to decide who you're going to rumba with. Your choices: *Sopranos* stallion **James Gandolfini** or *Godfather* goodfellas **Al Pacino** or **Robert De Niro**.

Ricky Martin, John Travolta, and **Patrick Swayze** all want to spin you around on the floor—in a nightclub and in the bedroom. But first decide who you'd do and then choose which of the following dirty dances you would have him do to you:

The Mean-Mattress Mambo
The Salsa Slip 'n' Slide
The Touch-You-Everywhere Tango Turn-on

DANCING MACHINE

You have thirty seconds to go through the following list and make your rapid-fire selections. Who would you do?

Pee-wee Herman or **Herman Munster**?

Jennifer Aniston or **Jennifer Jason Leigh**?

Tom Cruise or **Tom Hanks**?

Burt Reynolds or **Bert Convy**?

Marilyn Manson or **Charles Manson**?

Meg Ryan or **Ryan O'Neal**?

Richard Gere or **Richard Chamberlain**?

Hilary Swank or **Hillary Clinton**?

Larry King or **Billie Jean King**?

Sandra Bullock or **Sandra Day O'Connor**?

NAUGHTY NAME GAME

LAUGH RIOT

Who would you do: **Weird Al Yankovic** or **Carrot Top**?

CINEMATIC SEX SHOW

Which of these movie moments would you want to participate in: any sex scene from *The Big Easy* with **Ellen Barkin** and **Dennis Quaid**; **Jason Biggs** and the **pastry** from *American Pie*; the bit in *Ghost* when **Patrick Swayze** and **Demi Moore** make out over the pottery wheel; the tabletop scene in *The Postman Always Rings Twice* with **Jack Nicholson** and **Jessica Lange**; or the ménage à trois with **Matt Dillon, Denise Richards,** and **Neve Campbell** in *Wild Things*?

You've sampled all that Earth has to offer, and now it is time to reach for the stars— intergalactic nookie. Choose one experienced *Star Trek* explorer to take you where no one has gone before. As your guide, do you want the original, **Captain James T. Kirk** (William Shatner), *The Next Generation*'s **Captain Jean-Luc Picard** (Patrick Stewart), *Deep Space Nine*'s **Captain Benjamin Sisko** (Avery Brooks), *Voyager*'s **Captain Kathryn Janeway** (Kate Mulgrew), or *Enterprise*'s **Captain Jonathan Archer** (Scott Bakula)?

DIRTY PRIME DIRECTIVE

DATE DEBATE

The boss expects you to bring a date to the office Christmas party, and you want to make a good impression. Who do you invite and then, of course, drunkenly have sex with later: **Vanilla Ice** or **Andrew Dice Clay**?

NAME THAT
ORGASM

The **Vaccinator,** the **Passion Pincushion,** and the **Asian Lotus Lock** are all names of sex toys. Which would you want to try?

Capricorn can be teasing, taunting, and unbelievably fiery in the sack. In this speed round you have thirty seconds to pick your cosmic companions.

Taye Diggs or **Kevin Costner?**
Crystal Gayle or **Susan Lucci?**
Diane Sawyer or **Mary Tyler Moore?**
Hector Elizondo or **Jimmy Buffett?**
Chyna or **Chynna Phillips?**
John Amos or **Jim Carrey?**
Julia Ormond or **Julia Louis-Dreyfus?**
Chad Lowe or **Jason Bateman?**
Pat Benatar or **Jane Wyman?**
Michael Stipe or **Joan Baez?**

ASTROLOGICAL AROUSAL

All you want in life is a guy who can make you laugh. Well, **John Cleese, Terry Gilliam, Eric Idle, Terry Jones,** and **Michael Palin** are all happy to take a fun-loving tumble with you. Pick your Python passion.

MONTY
MISCHIEF

WHICH CICCONE

Let's be honest: we've all seen **Madonna** naked, so we know she has one booming system. But which Madonna reincarnation would you most want to do: **Material Girl, Spiritual Girl,** or **Cowgirl**?

VACATION SEX-ATHON

Both **Tony Curtis** and **Tony Danza** want to take you on a very special holiday—except there is no plan to leave the hotel room. Who do you say yes to?

DISAPPEARING ACTS

You are at your college graduation ceremony when suddenly your clothes start disappearing. First your pretty little cashmere twinset and your elegant ankle-length wool skirt dissolve. Then your black crotch-less panties and matching bra (with the extra-pert nipple insert) vanish. Is this a dream? No. You just realize that your old boyfriends **David Copperfield** and **David Blaine** have arrived and are both working a little magic to make your big day a special one. Who do you thank?

DUELING DIVAS

Celine Dion and **Mariah Carey** are begging to give you a private performance. Who are you going to help hit the high notes in the sack?

You've been invited to attend a neighborhood garden party that in addition to offering a nice game of croquet also includes some tasteful wife swapping. Which couple would you like to "visit" with first: **Michael Douglas** and **Catherine Zeta-Jones, John Stamos** and **Rebecca Romijn-Stamos,** or **Charlie Sheen** and **Denise Richards**?

SWINGERS

You're riding your big rig and you've got your hammer down when a message comes over the C.B. that the bandit **Burt Reynolds** and pal **Jerry Reed** want you to pull into the nearest weigh station for a dirty pit stop. Who gets the big 10-4 good buddy, and who gets nothing?

SMOKEY ON
YOUR TAIL?

DOG-EAT-DOG DILEMMA

You are starring in *Survivor* with **Bette Midler, Naomi Campbell,** and **Courtney Thorne-Smith,** but the group dynamic is simply not working. Who do you vote off the island? Who do you eat for sustenance? And who do you sleep with over and over again?

A little twitch of the nose and a small lusty spell could make any of these magical mavens yours. Who would you like to work your sorcery with: **Jeannie** from *I Dream of Jeannie*, **Samantha** from *Bewitched*, or any of the *Charmed* girls?

DO YOU BELIEVE IN MAGIC?

SHOOTIN' THE HOOPS

You're looking for the bathroom at a basketball game when you find that you've walked into the men's locker room instead. Everywhere you look you see glistening, muscular, *mucho grande* specimens of manhood—wearing absolutely nothing. The blood rushes from your head to, well, other recently activated locations, and you pass out cold on the floor. As you slowly come to, you find **Kobe Bryant** and **Shaquille O'Neal** standing over you, offering to help in any way they can. Who would you do?

TEEN DREAMS

The eighties were good to these ladies, and now they want to be good to you. Who would you do: **Ally Sheedy, Molly Ringwald, Phoebe Cates,** or **Demi Moore**?

PLANETARY PASSION

Which *Star Wars* royal would you like to have a steamy, lusty, racy, reckless, raunchy night with: **Princess Leia** (Carrie Fisher) or **Queen Amidala** (Natalie Portman)?

Aquarius takes the mind-body approach to sex. Imagine kissing with eyes open, hands stroking slowly, and thinking up new and exotic positions. You have twenty seconds to make your rapid-fire selections from this list of water babes.

Robby Benson or **Richard Dean Anderson?**
Bridget Fonda or **Lucinda Williams?**
Oral Roberts or **Rip Torn?**
Yoko Ono or **Vanessa Redgrave?**
Tom Selleck or **Tom Brokaw?**
Judith Light or **Tina Louise?**
Buzz Aldrin or **Ernest Borgnine?**
Portia de Rossi or **Christie Brinkley?**
Boris Yeltsin or **Garth Brooks?**
Mena Suvari or **Christina Ricci?**

ASTROLOGICAL AROUSAL

You've got cheap booze, Lynyrd Skynyrd on the stereo, and the two Tyler girls keeping you company. Who do you make out with first: **Liv Tyler** or **Mia Tyler**?

SISTER ACT

OOH, BABY

Some songs make you melt, and some singers? Well, they seem to embody sophisticated seduction. So who would you do: **Barry White** or **Luther Vandross**?

ARTISTIC EXPRESSION

Farrah Fawcett is ready to film her newest painting-in-the-buff video and wants you to be her model, but you're already booked that day helping **Richard Gere** build his all-nude Buddhist meditation retreat. Who do you assist?

Both **Oscar De La Hoya** and **George Foreman** become all achy and weak when they're around you. They send flowers, they write poems. They're desperate for even the smallest little dinner with you. Who do you say yes to?

ROCK 'EM, SOCK 'EM

UNIFORM NOOKIE

Aren't you the lucky one? It can be hard to meet a nice guy, and here you have more than A Few Good Men all hot and bothered for you. **Tom Cruise, Jack Nicholson, Kevin Bacon,** and **Keifer Sutherland** are ready to do your bidding. But who will you pick? (A tip: try to let the others down easy, because word has it that this crowd "can't handle the truth.")

The white zinfandel has been poured, the electric fireplace turned on, and your matching nylon nightie is oh-so-casually slipping from your shoulders. The only thing left to do is to choose your Romeo. Who'll it be: **John Tesh** or **Yanni**?

EASY LISTENING

EROTIC ICE

Both **Eric Heiden** and **Apolo Anton Ohno** want to play bare-naked skate-and-go-seek with you. Who do you do?

You are nothing but trouble. You smoke dope, you go clubbing all night, and you are very comfortable being photographed in the buff with your latest girlfriend. That's why you are a magnet for all the presidential daughters. The **Bush twins, Chelsea Clinton,** and even **Patti Davis** are after your bad self—but who do you choose?

POLITICAL
PASSIONS

CAPED CAROUSING AND CRUSADING

He's filthy rich, single, and looks great in leather—what's not to love? The only problem with pursuing Batman is that you've got to decide which one you want the most: **Adam West, Michael Keaton, Val Kilmer,** or **George Clooney**?

In order to make extra money, the little ladies of the subdivision have decided to perform in an upcoming strip show. Although all are practicing their lewd dances, only one woman gets to be the totally-naked-as-a-jaybird star of the night. Who do you most want to see strut her stuff in the buff: **Jenna Elfman, Helena Bonham Carter,** or **Shannen Doherty?**

THE FULL MONTY

You've taken a temp job for three months. Once you've made multiple international personal phone calls and stolen a nice selection of items from the supply closet, it's time to choose your screen saver. Unfortunately, you have only three options: nude photos of **Geraldo Rivera, James Earl Jones,** or **George Carlin**. Who do you pick?

SCREAM SCREEN

EYE CANDY

You are dating a sexy star who confesses that the only way she can reach orgasm is if you lick her eyeball. Who will you turn on with your tongue: **Carmen Electra, Bridget Fonda,** or **Minnie Driver**?

Those born under **Pisces** have a big appetite for sex—especially if it's with people they love. Think playful, think creative, think making whoopee in the hot tub. You have thirty seconds to select your favorite water babies.

Benicio Del Toro or **James Van Der Beek**?
Tammy Faye Bakker Messner or **Lynn Redgrave**?
Charley Pride or **Rob Lowe**?
Holly Hunter or **Téa Leoni**?
Spike Lee or **Neil Sedaka**?
Liza Minnelli or **Erik Estrada**?
William H. Macy or **Kelsey Grammer**?
Justine Bateman or **Jasmine Guy**?
Sam Donaldson or **Quincy Jones**?
Linda Fiorentino or **Chastity Bono**?

ASTROLOGICAL
AROUSAL

SHRINK UNWRAPPED

You know it's wrong, but you just can't say no to fifty solid minutes of boink therapy a week. But which psychiatrist will you choose to give you the full treatment? **Billy Crystal** (from *Analyze This*) or **Bob Newhart** (from *The Bob Newhart Show*)?

SCANDAL SCENARIO

You're a fresh-faced **White House intern** who's just arrived in D.C. with nothing in your suitcase but a thong and a new set of kneepads. The president invites you into the Oval Office and things really get smokin'—until you make the mistake of telling a trippy friend, who blabs to the press.

OR

You're a **pretty-boy member of the Brat Pack** with the harmless hobby of videotaping your bedroom trysts. And why not? It's just a fun little memento to keep revisiting when you're living in the actors' old-age home. Unfortunately, your latest lusty video leaks to the press, and your naked butt is everywhere.

Which scandal scenario would you choose?

In this ten-second speed round, pick the Hollywood High graduates who you would most want to educate after the alumni dinner.

Stefanie Powers or **Jill St. John**?
Charlene Tilton or **Linda Evans**?
Carole Lombard or **Fay Wray**?

FAST TIMES AT HOLLYWOOD HIGH

BIG BANG

We lied: size *does* matter. But legend has it that **Liam Neeson, David Duchovny,** and **Willem Dafoe** all sport, um, supersized packages—so they probably aren't concerned with this revelation. Which of these blessed boys would you like to tackle?

In which of the following frisky feature films would you like to play the erotic and inventive ingénue: *American Booty, Austin's Tower of Power,* or *The Talented Mister Titley*?

MOVIE-MATTRESS MAGIC

BED, BATH & BEYOND
YOUR WILDEST DREAMS

You've come home from a long, hard day at the office to find a bubble bath waiting, the room glowing with candles, and _____ holding a glass of wine for you. "Hi, Beautiful," he says in a deep, husky voice. "Let me take your clothes off, help you slip into the water, and then feed you grapes while reciting erotic poetry. After your bath, I'm going to dry you and lead you to our big, big bed, where I'll administer a modified Russian-Swedish deep-tissue massage. Then I'll make sweet, sweet love to you until the sun rises." **Denzel Washington, Bruce Springsteen, Derek Jeter,** and **Bono** all want to be your mystery man. Who do you choose to fill in your blank?

GROOVE ME, BABY

You're at a local dance club when **J. Lo** and **Lil' Kim** challenge you to a nude dance-off (with a guaranteed postcompetition make-out session). Who do you say yes to?

CREATE YOUR OWN EROTICA IN THREE EASY STEPS

1. Fill in the following blanks (without looking at the story on pages 174 and 175).

2. Insert these answers into the fun little tale on those pages.

3. Read the adventure aloud to amuse and arouse your friends.

City name

Male celebrity name

Item of clothing

Body-part name

Body-part name

Body-part name

Female celebrity name

Sex-position name

Body-part name

Body-part name

Favorite curse word

Old-fashioned expression (example: Golly gee whiz)

Room in a house

Dance name (example: the Electric Slide)

Exclamation

CREATE YOUR OWN EROTICA (CONT.)

You are a transvestite waitress working in a fill in city name hotel bar, saving your tips for a sex change. One night you notice fill in male celebrity name sitting in your section. You check yourself out in the mirror, adjust your fill in clothing item name to hide your fill in body-part name, fix your fake fill in body-part name, and brush your fill in body-part name–length blond hair, then make your way over.

"What would you like to have?" you ask in your breathiest fill in female celebrity name voice.

"I'll have a fill in sexual position name straight up," he says in a gruff voice, as he leans in and gets a smell of your fill in body-part name, his eyes trailing down your body and resting on your fill in body-part name.

"Anything else with that?" you say, and no sooner are the words out than you feel his hand slipping up your thigh. His touch is electric.

When he reaches your most tender spot, you say, "fill in curse word."

He says, "fill in old-fashioned expression." And then he says, "Let's go back to my fill in room name and do the fill in dance name till we can only say fill in exclamation."

Now that you've answered each and every one of the previous salacious and scintillating questions (which have been thoughtfully created for you by a trained professional), you're ready, really ready to put your dirty mind to work. **List your own favorite combinations here:**

Partner No. 1:

Partner No. 2:

Sexual Scenario:

THE TRAINING WHEELS ARE OFF

LIST YOUR OWN COMBINATION HERE

Partner No. 1:

Partner No. 2:

Sexual Scenario:

THE TRAINING WHEELS ARE OFF
LIST YOUR OWN COMBINATION HERE

Partner No. 1:

Partner No. 2:

Sexual Scenario:

THE TRAINING WHEELS ARE OFF
LIST YOUR OWN COMBINATION HERE

Partner No. 1:

Partner No. 2:

Sexual Scenario:

THE TRAINING WHEELS ARE OFF
LIST YOUR OWN COMBINATION HERE

Partner No. 1:

Partner No. 2:

Sexual Scenario:

THE TRAINING WHEELS ARE OFF
LIST YOUR OWN COMBINATION HERE

Partner No. 1:

Partner No. 2:

Sexual Scenario:

THE TRAINING WHEELS ARE OFF
LIST YOUR OWN COMBINATION HERE

About the Author

Susan Segrest is a freelance writer and editor in New
York City. She has been an editor at *Cosmopolitan,*
Marie Claire, Mode, and *New Woman* and has written
for many other publications, including *Fitness, Reader's*
Digest, and the New York *Daily News.* She has also
worked for a film company in London, the U.S.
Senate, and numerous all-you-can-eat barbecue
shacks. She can be reached via her website,
www.who-would-you-do.com.